In my heart of hearts, I know, have known, and always will know who and what I am, where I'm from, that I'm here in this changing frequency for a while to live learn experience and bring at least some of the infinite love I know so well in my heart of hearts.

I wrote this book over the course of three years, from 2019 to 2022. Many of the photos and poems came from a time when I lived mostly alone, with my two parents, in the suburbs of New Jersey (as well as New Mexico briefly in 2020 & South America in late 2021-2022). There I spent the majority of my time in the woods, in churches, cafes, libraries, or diners to pass the time and stay warm during the cold seasons. It took all my strength and willingness to surrender my need for external stimulation or connection with other people to be able to exist peacefully and connect to myself at that time. May it inspire you in and through whatever time you may be going through as you read this. Thank you for reading.

Chapter 1: Into the Wild

Exploring Infinity as a cell in Nature's body...

Nature is a reflection of the Glory within us.

Nature is a reflection of Who We Truly Are.

My Name

I wandered back
Into that old prison
A relapse
To find an old vision
What I found
Was a corpse on the ground
Wet sweaty bloody chains
And the sky
Glorious
Stretching forever
My name.

Great Hands

When great hands come upon you
What do you do?
Do you run?
Do you hide?
Do you curl up,
And hope to die?
When greater hands come upon you
And you cannot run
And you cannot hide
I sit
Until every struggling part of me
Dies.

And I,
The dreamer of this dream
Survive.

Your **S**on

-

Your son
Was born
From your womb
Was born
From your semen
Walked this Earth
Made friends
Laughed and cried a lot
Felt insecure at times
Glimpsed who he is
Drifted back into self-pity
Remembered
Wrote a poetry book
And forgot
Only to do it all over again.

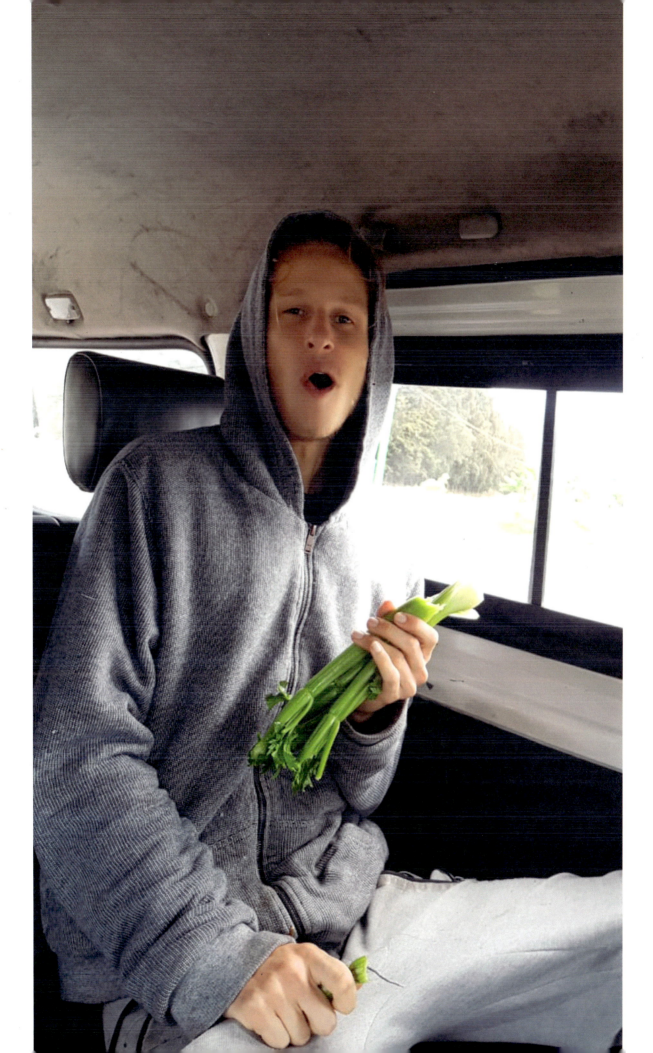

The first step out of suffering is accepting where you are exactly as you are.

Battles

Some of the greatest battles
Are fought
Within your own mind
And heart
In a raging silence
No one can hear
But you.

Allow yourself to grow with observation, appreciation, and invitation, not condemnation.

Why I Garden, Why I Pray

Wrestling in the dark
To find my way to Truth
Memories coming up
To be seen and then moved thru

Food addiction,
Wasting away
Why I garden
Why I pray
Why I eat
And why I don't
Praying for guidance
But hoping I won't
Surrendering
So I don't stuff my face
The real hunger
Deep down
Is the same
For the entire human race.

You must face yourself
In a million masks
Before you see
Your True Face.

Divine Fusion/Life

I looked at loneliness
I felt it
And realized
It was only an illusion
How could you ever be lonely
When everything exists already
In Divine Fusion?

There is nothing to be earned
Nothing to be gained
Except a life lived
A blessing all the same.

Spiritual Growth

Is something

That happens

Silently

Quietly

In the quantum cracking

Of your soul

It happens

It happens

It happens.

(Dis)Connection

-

When I go
Into Nature
The devils and angels
Leave me alone
And I sit
On a baseless throne
I realize
Either I must be immortal
Or I'll lose everything and everyone
I've ever known
Then I go into Nature
And realize
This is the way things are.
The trees aren't afraid
Why is it just humans
That need immortality?

Forest...life...trillions of organisms growing, dying, breathing, in and around us

-

And then we try to control it.

Chapter 2: The Wild Abyss

Milk and Honey

In the right octave
These words go down
Fine
Like milk and honey
Please savor
These words now
And don't wait til later
To hold my prayers.

Mountains

Times when I feel dead

And alone

I look at the mountains

And sing my song

Forgive me, forgive me

I've already

Come home.

Wild

I long for
Far out places
Warm embraces
Cuddles by the fire
By fire lit places
I wish for the vastness
Of my aloneness
Just me and the mountains
And (K)no(w)-ledge.

The Trees

Teach me
I am
Where I'm meant to be

Teach me
I am
Who I'm meant to be

Teach me
I am going
Where I'm meant to be going

Teach me
How to always be free
To be me.

Even if I'm force-fed Fritos
In a penitentiary!

Of Gaia

I am of the desert
I roar like the sea
I am of the plant kingdom
You are one of me
I am of the ocean
The sky the birds, the mean
Preying machine
Praying to be free one day
With me
No slave masters
I am free
I am free
I am free

If you don't know your darkness then your light is like a wisping candle ready to be blown out at the next vicissitude of life.

Surrender

Sometimes
My heart hurts so bad
I go into the forest
Open my mind
And let Life (w)in.

Wind, Earth, Fire, Flame

Wind, Earth
Fire, Flame
When you die
This Earth
Calls your name
When you die
You go Home
When you die
How stupid to think
You're all alone.

Feeling Unfelt Feelings

Feeling unfelt feelings

Can be hard

It's like

Digging into

Unhealed scars

But this is what you're made for

This is what

You're bred for

Unhealed

You heal

And the Universe

Comes back into balance.

Why?

Does the bee
Question why
It gathers honey

Does the bird
Question why
It feeds its babies

Does the human
Question why
Why?

It's only a question -

When life flows
It's only
An answer.

Day by day

Moment by moment

I live life.

We Walk

-

I guess we walk in this darkness
Alone
Yet we still
Guide, follow,
And at times
Hold each other
Yet we're alone
Alone together
We walk.

Soul Water Part 2

-

Where will you go
When your thoughts
Fly endlessly by
From where will you drink
When every idea
Is another shuttering goodbye
Not a soul in this world
Knows the pain you endure
Mindfucking a way
To keep the world alive
I know there's no clean water
But I don't mind
I'm dying because
The soul water's
Run dry.

Maybe it's just

The bruises and the shocks

From when I thought

This world was Real and it was Not.

THE PEOPLE
THAT WALKED
IN DARKNESS
HAVE SEEN A
GREAT LIGHT

Divine Voice

Who am I to judge
What another person eats

Who am I to tell another
To release all their pain
When I have not yet done the same?

Who's another
To do the same

Who are we
When we have no choice?

Purely, Only, the Divine Voice.

Being Human

I know sometimes
It's hard to be human
I know sometimes
It's hard
To let your darkness go
I know
So here's a phrase
Love yourself
(Always &) Anyways.

Silence

Only when
Your silence
Empties you
And your emptiness
Breaks you
Will you be ready
For a life
In the Spirit.

Memory

You will feel like you are
About to die
You will feel as though
You are being
Burned alive
And you will
Breathe
Into the fire
Remembering
Your heartbeat
As God's.

The Human Journey

-

You will walk

Into the desert

Of your own heart

And you will stumble

You will wish to be carried

By mirages

And you will walk

And be carried

Into the Mecca

Of your own heart.

-

And I will meet you there.

You Are Too Far

I suffer because

I think what should be

Is different from what is

I play this game

And it drives me insane

What is,

Is

Isn't it?

-

All you project

Will tear you apart

Know in your heart

Everything it destroys

Is not who you are

You are greater

And will always be

Too far.

You are too far
You have grown
And come to
Where you are
Now from here
Go
As you are
An Eternal, Infinite
Star.

I know who you are in Truth
I know what you are in Truth
I know how you serve in Truth
You are free, you are free,
You are Free.

To Lee, thank you and keep up the good work.

Thank you to Nature
& Yeni

Amen.

Made in the USA
Columbia, SC
13 June 2024

36906426R00049